My mother's gifts

My mother's gifts

A celebration of motherly love

RYLAND
PETERS
& SMALL
LONDON NEW YORK

Senior Designer Megan Smith

Senior Editor Clare Double

Picture Research Tracy Ogino

Production Gemma Moules

Art Director Anne-Marie Bulat

Editorial Director Julia Charles

Publishing Director Alison Starling

First published in the
United States in 2006
by Ryland Peters & Small
519 Broadway, 5th Floor
New York, NY 10012
www.rylandpeters.com

10 9 8 7 6 5 4 3 2 1

Text, design, and photographs
© Ryland Peters & Small 2006
Photograph on page 45
© Steve Painter

ISBN-10: 1-84597-197-3
ISBN-13: 978-1-84597-197-7

Printed and bound in China

Contents

Introduction

Mothers pass on so much more than mere genes to their children. They shape us in myriad ways, many of which we don't really appreciate until we are fully grown, and perhaps have our own children. Often we unconsciously echo our mothers in our gestures, phrases, and even the way we laugh or walk, and we find ourselves remembering her philosophical words in times of adversity. This book is a reflection of that shared experience.

Although the words here belong to individual mothers and their families, they contain much useful advice on finding one's way in the world, overcoming doubt or disappointment, and making the most of the good times, too. The gift of good counsel must be universal to all mothers.

We'd like to thank everyone who shared their stories and reflections with us, and of course give a hearty thank you to their mothers.

Wisdom

The price of wisdom is above rubies. BIBLE, JOB 28:18

All the times I felt "I should have known," my mother reminded me that hindsight is the worst possible birth defect.

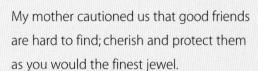

My mother cautioned us that good friends are hard to find; cherish and protect them as you would the finest jewel.

My mother always led me to believe that being female was no bar to success in life—and that there was no reason why I could not achieve whatever I desired. Her greatest gift to me was self-belief, which is something I have tried to pass on to my own children.

"Keep your eye on the doughnut, not the hole." Concentrate on what you have, not what is missing.

My mother
always told us:
"Don't be envious of
what others have, for you
don't know how they got it." Now that I am
older, I am aware of the truth of this and
am very grateful for the little that I do have.

My mother taught me that life isn't fair—but
sometimes that will be to your advantage.

Nothing ever stays the same. New doors will always
open for you—usually when you least expect it.

You don't get wiser with age, you just get better
at covering up what you don't know!

Beware false economies. In most aspects of life, you will get what you pay for.

If you're not where you want to be today, keep putting one foot in front of the other and you'll get there, one step at a time.

As an overweight teenager I suffered from a chronic lack of self-confidence. My mother told me to stop worrying about what others thought of me and to concentrate instead on what *I* thought about *them*, sound advice that's stood me in good stead throughout my adult life.

The hand that rocks the cradle
Is the hand that rules the world.

W. R. WALLACE

Strength

My mother taught
me that age is most
definitely an attitude,
and not to be held back
by what other people
think you should be
doing in your life.

"Stand up straight!" This was the clarion cry of my mother, who hated poor posture—not only because it's bad for your back, but because good posture is an easy way to look more elegant, confident, and even slimmer. I think what she really meant is that if you stand up straight and look others in the eye, they will treat you as an equal, and you will respect yourself.

Finding an extra pinch of strength was a specialty of my mother's. As she said, if you can find something to laugh about, things can't be all bad. (And there's always *something* to laugh about.)

My mother gave me the courage to pursue my dreams, making me believe in myself and that I could achieve anything I put my mind to, as long as I worked hard enough.

When my mother went away for her work as a
sales rep, I stayed with my grandmother. I missed
Mom very much at night and often I couldn't get
to sleep. Mom told me that when I missed her
I should look out of the window at the night sky
and find the brightest star. She said that she would
also look for it at my bedtime, and it would reassure
both of us. The star would always be in the sky,
even if Mom was on another continent. I still look
up occasionally and remember how looking at the
stars comforted me. Now that I'm an adult, star-gazing
still gives me a feeling of immense calm.

When I was grieving over my separation from a
boyfriend and agonizing over whether it could have
worked out or not, my mother's remedy was to say,
"Oh love, write his name on a list and cross it off."
Sometimes you just have to accept that things are
the way they are, but a little decisive action can help
you feel more in control of the situation.

26 my mother's gifts

Security

A mother is a mother still,
The holiest thing alive.

SAMUEL TAYLOR COLERIDGE

She instilled in me "Neither a borrower nor a lender be"—not to be beholden to anyone. I have found that it is better to give rather than lend. Lending destroys relationships.

My mother always said in reference to possessions that "You can't take it with you." She felt you should not place too much store on things, as in the end you leave them behind.

Don't have any regrets about the past, only new plans for the future.

When I was a child my mother always did her best to make me feel cherished and safe. I still remember the sensation of being snuggled in a terry cloth beach robe after a cold swim in the sea or the importance of a favorite bedtime story at the end of a busy day at school. My mother still makes me feel calm and loved and I hope to give that to my own daughter as she grows up. It's a great foundation for life.

My mother has always advocated that all you can do is to do your best. She would never get cross if we didn't get the marks we were expecting from exams, and was proud no matter what. That's always stayed with me; she's never made me feel like a failure.

Now that I am a mother myself, I am trying to figure out what makes my mother so good at the job. She has always had interests outside the home—work, friends, and long games of tennis—but managed to make her three children feel that they were the center of her universe (without ever playing the martyr). Mothers need to be both a lively, independent role model for the grown-up world yet to come, and also an endlessly patient, nurturing, and loving figure for the fleeting years of childhood. Looking back, I think she got it just right.

Each day is a new beginning—a gift. My mother would say that there are many people who didn't wake up this morning, and you should take each day as the first day of the rest of your life.

You should always have a fabulous lipstick in your bag, a great book on the go, and a pot full of running-away money (in case you have to implement plan B).

Never rely on anyone else for your sense of self. It's only when you are your own person that you can truly connect with someone else.

Most folks are about as
happy as they make up their
minds to be. ABRAHAM LINCOLN

Happiness

When I was growing up my mother always said,
"Live for today and tomorrow will look after itself."
At that time, it helped me dismiss worries that
I might have about scary events that were coming
up—such as starting a new school. Now that I am
a mother, it reminds me to enjoy every moment
that I have with my son and not to worry about
the future, but to look forward.

Some good comes of
everything, even if you
can't see what it is at
the time.

Make your own fate: think positively and good things will happen.

My mother taught me that you can choose to be happy, but that it requires action. After all, that knight in shining armor won't find you if you don't make it out of the house.

When I was desolate over breaking up with someone who hadn't treated me well, my mother said: "That's not love, love is something that makes you happy."

One of the delights of my childhood was sitting in my
nightgown watching my mother get ready to go out
for the evening. It was the seventies, so her dresses
were long, bright, and plunging. I loved the intimacy
of the event and watching the transformation of
everyday Mommy into a glamorous creature in
evening shoes. Now I realize that she would have
found it much more relaxing to get ready alone,
so I appreciate those moments even more.

Years ago my heart was broken when the friend I had fallen in love with didn't feel the same. My mother counseled me to keep the friendship and see how my own feelings changed over time. Now he's married, and I count him and his wife among my closest friends and enjoy happy times with them and their baby son.

My mother instilled a love of reading in me as she read me bedtime stories and, later on, gave me the books that she had loved as a child. I think of her when I read favorite books to my own children and when they enjoy the same stories that she and I enjoyed together. A book can still transport me from everyday problems.

Love

Love sought is good, but giv'n unsought is better.

WILLIAM SHAKESPEARE

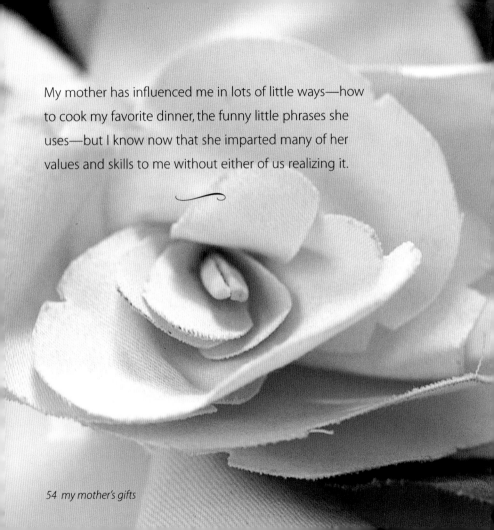

My mother has influenced me in lots of little ways—how to cook my favorite dinner, the funny little phrases she uses—but I know now that she imparted many of her values and skills to me without either of us realizing it.

My mother accepts the worst things about me and still loves me in spite of my flaws and idiosyncrasies. She is always there with a box of tissues or a much-needed cooked dinner. After all, there is nothing like a mother to comfort you, whether it is with food or just love.

It's important to like yourself and treat yourself as well as you treat other people. Pay attention to your clothes and hair, because if you feel good on the outside, it will help you feel good on the inside.

My mother taught me that just because one
man breaks your heart, it doesn't mean no one
else loves you.

My mother taught me to be generous in matters of
the heart, even when the love is coming to an end. I
had already bought some (expensive) concert tickets
for both of us when my boyfriend and I broke up. She
advised me to treat the night out as his severance
pay! I learned that it's best to part amicably, if you can.

I know I can always ask my mother for a hug and
a cuddle. She never turns me down!

No matter how complicated life got when I was growing up, we found a way through it, and my mother put me first every time. She always made it seem so easy. When I was a child we used to watch the Sunday afternoon movie together. I particularly loved the musicals, and one weekend she taught me how to dance. We had so much fun waltzing around the living room to *The King and I*, and even now the thought makes me smile.

Picture credits

Key: ph=photographer, a=above, b=below, r=right, l=left, c=center

Endpapers ph Catherine Gratwicke; **1** ph Dan Duchars;
2–3 background ph Claire Richardson; **3 inset** ph David Loftus;
4 ph Polly Wreford; **5** ph Claire Richardson; **7** ph Jan Baldwin;
8–9l ph Polly Wreford; **9c** ph Alan Williams; **9r** ph Simon Upton;
10–11 ph Dan Duchars; **12–13** ph Polly Wreford; **14** ph Debi Treloar;
15 ph Dan Duchars; **16a** ph Polly Wreford; **16b** ph Catherine Gratwicke;
17 ph Daniel Farmer; **18** ph Jan Baldwin; **19l** ph Chris Tubbs;
19c & r ph James Merrell; **20–21** ph Polly Wreford; **22** ph Dan Duchars;
23 ph Melanie Eclare; **24** ph Catherine Gratwicke; **26–27** ph James Merrell;
28 ph Daniel Farmer; **29l & c** ph James Merrell; **29r** ph Polly Wreford;
30 ph Sandra Lane; **31–32** ph Christopher Drake; **33** ph Caroline Arber;

Acknowledgments

Key: a=above, b=below, c=center

The publisher would like to thank our contributors, who made this book possible:

Anonymous Louise Alexander, page 54 **Donna Brown**, page 13
Julia Charles, pages 16b, 50 **Cornelia Coan Herlihy**, page 10a
Patricia Flahaven Dickson, page 10c **Mimi Flynn**, page 12
Sarah Fraser, pages 22b, 25, 56a, 60 **Annabel Morgan**, page 51
Alison Starling, pages 33, 37, 49 **Monica Taitt**, page 38a
Nikki Thresher, page 42 **Rosemary Van Wyk Smith**, page 30a and c
Rowena Westhead, pages 34, 59b **Liz Wilde**, page 20